D0624319

THE HISTORY OF THE SAN DIEGO CHARGERS

THE HISTORY OF THE
SAN DIEGO

Published by Creative Education

123 South Broad Street

Mankato, Minnesota 56001

Creative Education is an imprint of The Creative Company.

DESIGN AND PRODUCTION BY **EVANSDAY DESIGN**

LIBRARY OF CONGRESS CATALOGING-IN-PUBLICATION DATA

Schmalzbauer, Adam.

The history of the San Diego Chargers / by Adam Schmalzbauer.

p. cm. — (NFL today)

Summary: Highlights the key personalities and memorable games in the history
of San Diego's professional football team.

ISBN 978-1-58341-312-8

1. San Diego Chargers (Football team)—History—Juvenile literature.

[1. San Diego Chargers (Football team)—History. 2. Football—History.]

I. Title. II. Series.

GV956.S29S36 2004

796.332'64'09794985—dc22   2003063096

9 8 7 6 5

COVER PHOTO: running back LaDainian Tomlinson

SAN DIEGO IS THE SECOND-LARGEST CITY IN CALIFORNIA AND IS LOCATED ON THE SAN DIEGO BAY IN THE SOUTHWESTERN PART OF THE STATE. FOUNDED BY SPANISH MISSIONARIES IN 1769, SAN DIEGO WAS SEIZED BY MEXICO IN 1822. IT LATER CAME UNDER THE CONTROL OF THE UNITED STATES DURING THE MEXICAN WAR, OFFICIALLY BECOMING A U.S. CITY IN 1850. TODAY, THIS BEAUTIFUL PORT CITY IS HOME TO MORE THAN ONE MILLION PEOPLE—AND ONE NATIONAL FOOTBALL LEAGUE (NFL) TEAM: THE SAN DIEGO CHARGERS. ORIGINALLY FORMED IN LOS ANGELES IN 1959, THE CHARGERS STARTED OUT AS AN AMERICAN FOOTBALL LEAGUE (AFL) FRANCHISE. THE CHARGERS WERE DECKED OUT IN SHARP-LOOKING UNIFORMS OF BLUE AND GOLD, COMPLETE WITH LIGHTNING BOLTS ON THE HELMETS AND PANTS, BUT L.A. FANS WERE LESS THAN ENTHUSIASTIC ABOUT THE NEW TEAM. SO, IN 1961, THE CHARGERS MOVED DOWN THE CALIFORNIA COAST TO SAN DIEGO AND HAVE BEEN THERE EVER SINCE.

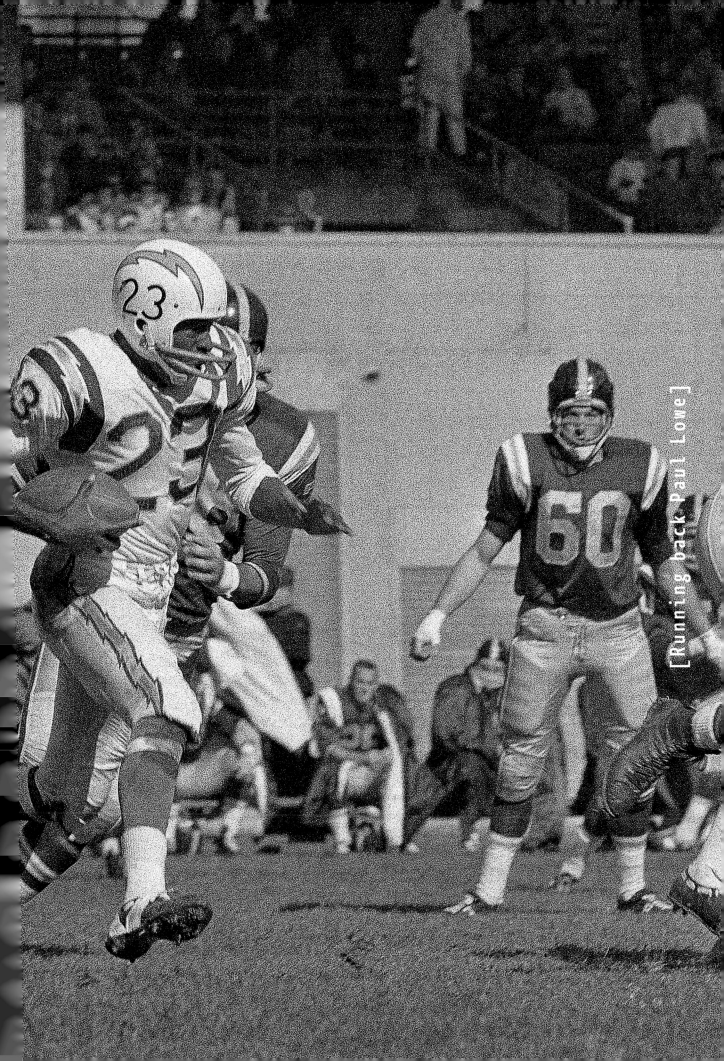

[Running back Paul Lowe]

CHARGING OUT OF THE GATE>

BEFITTING A TEAM with a lightning-bolt logo, the Chargers electrified their fans from the start. The team's first coach, Sid Gillman, had previously won an NFL championship while coaching the Los Angeles Rams, and he intended to lead the Chargers to championship glory as well. With a talented roster led by running back Paul Lowe and quarterback Jack Kemp, the Chargers went 10–4 in 1960 and won the AFL's Western Division in their only season in Los Angeles. Although they lost to the Houston Oilers in the AFL championship game, the good times were just beginning.

In 1961, the team moved to San Diego and surrounded Lowe and Kemp with more talent by drafting running back Keith Lincoln and defensive linemen Earl Faison and Ernie Ladd. These players carried the Chargers to another Western Division title. Unfortunately, the Oilers again topped the Chargers for the AFL championship.

Looking for a boost that would finally push the team to the top, Coach Gillman traded for a quick and sure-handed receiver named Lance Alworth in 1962. In 1963, Alworth—nicknamed "Bambi" because of his deer-like grace and energy—gave the team that boost by posting 1,206 receiving yards and scoring 11 touchdowns. With Alworth and two new quarterbacks, veteran Tobin Rote and youngster John Hadl, sparking the AFL's most explosive passing attack, San Diego crushed the Denver Broncos in the last game of the season to win its division yet again.

San Diego fans rejoiced as the Chargers then finally won their first AFL championship, demolishing the Boston Patriots 51–10. In that game, the Chargers offense was nearly unstoppable, and Lincoln blasted through the Patriots' defense for a whopping 206 rushing yards. "This isn't a football team," said awestruck Boston coach Mike Hovak. "It's a machine."

Quarterback John Hadl helped propel the Chargers of the '60s to three AFL championship games

The Chargers "machine" continued to run at full throttle in 1964 and 1965. San Diego returned to the AFL championship game both years, only to lose to the Buffalo Bills both times. Alworth and Hadl continued their offensive heroics, but the departure of Ladd in 1965 and Faison in 1966 hurt the team. Over the next three seasons, San Diego put together mediocre records. The Chargers had lost their championship luster.

FLYING HIGH AGAIN>

IN 1970, THE AFL and NFL merged, beginning a new

era in professional football. In their 10 AFL seasons, the

Chargers had won five division titles and one league

championship. But the team had grown old. In 1970, even

the greats failed to put up great numbers, as Alworth's

production dropped off and Hadl completed fewer than

half of his passes for the first time in eight seasons.

After the 1971 season, Sid Gillman stepped down as the

team's coach.

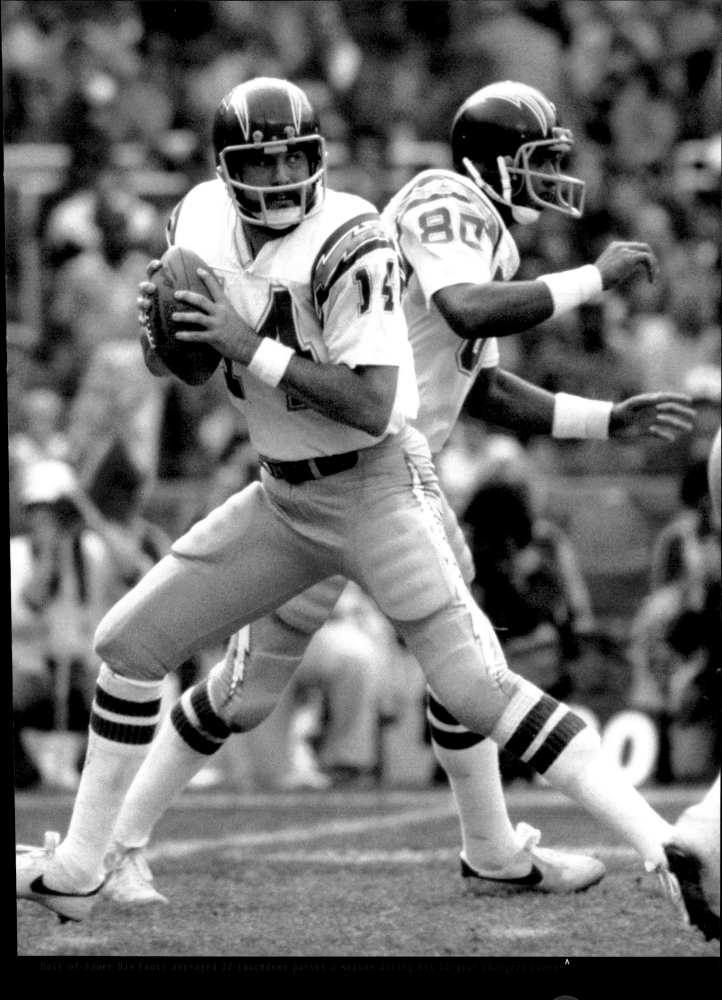

Hall-of-Famer Dan Fouts averaged 17 touchdown passes a season during his 15-year Chargers career.

With brilliant coach Don Coryell on the sidelines, San Diego made the playoffs for four straight seasons.

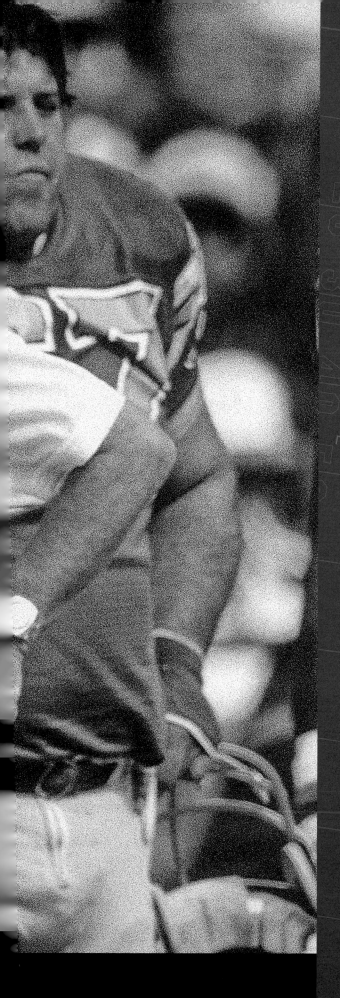

Despite some great efforts from running back Cid Edwards, tight end Pettis Norman, and terrifying defensive end Deacon Jones, the Chargers struggled for most of the 1970s. It wasn't until 1978 that they finally achieved their first winning season (9–7) of the decade. That year, Don Coryell stepped in as the club's new head coach in midseason and turned things around, leading the Chargers to seven victories in their final eight games.

Coach Coryell deserved much of the credit for the Chargers' sudden success, but so did new quarterback Dan Fouts. In 1979, the young passer from the University of Oregon exploded onto the scene by passing for 4,082 yards, setting a new NFL single-season record. This amazing performance helped propel the Chargers to a 12–4 record and their first division title since 1965. With Fouts leading Coryell's brilliant pass-oriented offense, sportswriters began calling the Chargers' passing attack "Air Coryell."

Behind Don and Dan, San Diego began to look like the Chargers of old. From 1979 to 1981, the team won the American Football Conference (AFC) Western Division title every year and posted a combined 33–15 record. The spark to this success was Fouts. In 1981, the quarterback that many considered the toughest in the NFL broke his own

Jackie Gary "Big Hands" Johnson was a fierce pass rusher, making a team record 17.5 sacks in 1980.

single-season passing record for the third straight year, throwing for a whopping 4,802 yards and 33 touchdowns.

Unfortunately, the biggest prize of all eluded the Chargers, who could never quite reach the Super Bowl. In 1981, the team lost in the AFC championship game for the second straight season, despite having a loaded roster that included Pro Bowl defensive linemen Gary "Big Hands" Johnson, Louie Kelcher, and Fred Dean. "I can't tell you how much it hurts to come this far and lose two years in a row," Coach Coryell said sadly after the 1981 playoff loss to the Cincinnati Bengals.

CONSTANT CHARLIE>

UNDER THE CONSTANT push of Coach Coryell, the Chargers made the playoffs again in 1982, only to fall to the Miami Dolphins in the second round. The team's defense was dealt a terrible blow after the season when Johnson, Kelcher, and Dean all left town. Then, as they had a decade earlier, the Chargers slipped into a losing slump that would last most of the decade.

As injuries began to slow down Fouts, receiver Charlie Joiner remained one of the few consistent bright spots for San Diego during these years. At 5-foot-11 and 185 pounds, Joiner was rather small by NFL standards, but he made up for it with a powerful mixture of instincts and toughness. Called "the most intelligent receiver the game has ever known" by legendary San Francisco 49ers coach Bill Walsh, Joiner quietly posted four 1,000-yard

In his finest San Diego season (1981), steady receiver Charlie Joiner made 70 catches for 1,188 yards.

With his darting moves and sure hands, receiver Wes Chandler was a big-play threat for the Chargers.

Leslie O'Neal was the best pass rusher in club history ^

Tight end Kellen Winslow averaged 60 catches a year ^

seasons over the course of an amazing 18-year NFL career. Before he finally retired in 1987 at the age of 39, he would catch 750 passes for 12,146 yards—both NFL records.

Although the Chargers of the '80s featured other outstanding passing targets—including star tight end Kellen Winslow and receivers John Jefferson and Wes Chandler—the one constant link was Joiner. "I don't recall him ever missing a practice at all since I've been in San Diego," Coach Coryell said. "One time, he cracked a rib and didn't take a day off. He said, 'I'll work through it.'"

Except for the efforts of Joiner and his fellow receivers, the mid-1980s were some dark seasons for San Diego. In 1986, the team found a new defensive star as rookie end Leslie O'Neal made 12.5 quarterback sacks. The Chargers started 8–1 a year later but stumbled down the stretch and missed the playoffs again. Fouts and Winslow retired after that, leaving San Diego fans to hope for better things in the 1990s.

BEATHARD BRINGS THE BOLTS BACK>

AFTER FINISHING DEAD last in the AFC West in 1989,

San Diego hired a new general manager it believed could

ignite the "Bolts" once again: Bobby Beathard. Widely

considered one of the smartest men in the NFL, Beathard

had been responsible a decade earlier for rebuilding the

Washington Redskins. Chargers management hoped he

would work a similar miracle in San Diego.

Beathard quickly proved his genius by selecting line-

backer Junior Seau out of the University of Southern

California with San Diego's top pick in the 1990 NFL

Draft. An incredibly powerful player who could bench-

press 500 pounds, Seau became an instant terror in the

NFL and the heart of San Diego's defense. Bill Belichick,

the head coach of the Cleveland Browns, was astounded

by the Chargers' new star. "Junior Seau is the best defen-

sive player we've faced, I'd say, by a pretty good margin,"

said Belichick.

With his nose for the ball and incredible strength, Junior Seau anchored the defense for 13 seasons.

Workhorse Natrone Means carried the ball a team record 343 times during his great 1994 season.

After San Diego posted losing records in 1990 and 1991, Beathard continued to rebuild. In 1992, he hired a new head coach: Bobby Ross, who had just led Georgia Tech University to the national college championship. Beathard then picked up a new quarterback by signing former Washington Redskins signal-caller Stan Humphries. With these new pieces added to the puzzle, the 1992 Chargers made a startling comeback, winning their first AFC West title in more than a decade with an 11–5 record.

The team slipped to 8–8 in 1993 but charged back to 11–5 and another division title in 1994, thanks in part to the powerful running of rookie ball-carrier Natrone Means. Means set a club record that season with 1,350 rushing yards, while Humphries passed for 3,209 more to give the Chargers a well-balanced attack. The joy ride continued in San Diego as the Chargers beat the Miami Dolphins and Pittsburgh Steelers in two thrilling playoff games to win the AFC championship and reach their first Super Bowl. Seau, Means, and the rest of the Chargers would fall just short of an NFL championship, though, losing to the San Francisco 49ers 49–26.

RECHARGING FOR THE FUTURE>

THE CHARGERS MADE another run to the playoffs in 1995, but the season ended in disappointment with a 35–20 loss to the Indianapolis Colts. The Chargers had once again peaked without winning it all. Seau and such players as receiver Tony Martin continued to shine, but it wasn't enough. The Bolts went 8–8 in 1996, then crashed to the AFC West cellar again, finishing the 1997 season 4–12.

Determined to build the team back up with youth, Beathard and the Chargers traded two veteran players and what amounted to two seasons' worth of draft choices to the Arizona Cardinals for the right to the second overall pick in the 1998 NFL Draft. With it, San Diego selected Ryan Leaf, a promising, 6-foot-5 quarterback out of Washington State University. Hoping that Leaf would lead the team forward after adjusting to the pro game, the Chargers and their fans waited...and waited.

Speedy receiver Tony Martin tied an NFL record with a 99 yard touchdown reception in 1994.

Star halfback LaDainian Tomlinson had it all—great hands, surprising power, and breakaway speed.

Leaf never emerged as the star the team needed, and the Chargers continued to fade. After an embarrassing 1–15 season in 2000, San Diego released the quarterback.

After going through three coaches in four rocky seasons, San Diego hired veteran NFL coach Marty Schottenheimer to take charge of the team in 2002. Although the Chargers had gone just 5–11 the year before, Schottenheimer inherited a team with potential. In the 2001 NFL Draft, the Chargers had used the fifth overall pick to grab LaDainian Tomlinson, a powerful running back out of Texas Christian University. They had also drafted a tough young quarterback named Drew Brees.

Behind Coach Schottenheimer's leadership and the great play of Tomlinson—who charged for 1,375 rushing yards—the 2002 Chargers proved that they were no longer pushovers. By the end of the season, the team was 8–8 and had given its fans reasons for optimism. Although the San Diego faithful were saddened when 12-time Pro-Bowler Junior Seau left town after the season, they were encouraged by Tomlinson's emergence as one of the NFL's most dangerous running backs. "I've never coached a running back that has the kind of explosive change of direction he's got," Schottenheimer said of the young star. "He's got the ability to see

A quick and strong pass defender, cornerback Quentin Jammer was one of the league's fast-rising stars.

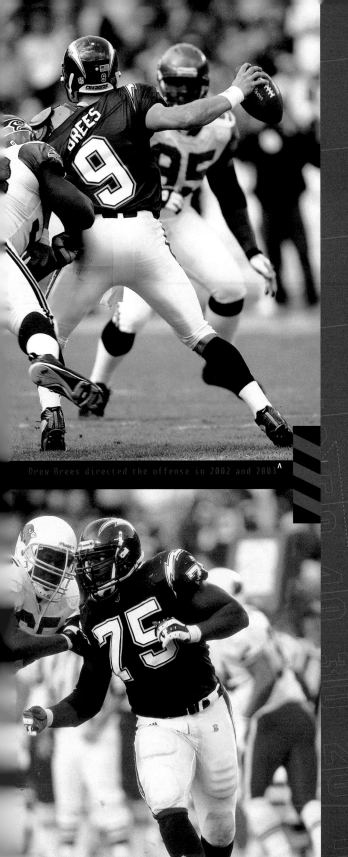

Drew Brees directed the offense in 2002 and 2003 ^

End Marcellus Wiley was a fierce pass rusher ^

things and make cuts that a lot of the winning running backs in this league don't have."

Although the Bolts stumbled to a disappointing 4–12 finish in 2003, things were looking sunny in San Diego. Besides Brees and the hard-charging Tomlinson, the Chargers featured such rising stars as cornerback Quentin Jammer, linebacker Ben Leber, and mammoth (6-foot-6 and 353 pounds) offensive tackle Courtney Van Buren. With Coach Schottenheimer guiding this new generation of heroes in blue and gold, the future looked bright.

From the glory days of the early 1960s, to the "Air Coryell" era, to the Super Bowl season of 1994, the team with the lightning bolt logo has earned its share of AFL and NFL success over the past four decades. From Alworth and Hadl to Fouts and Seau, San Diego has also been represented by some of the greatest players ever to wear cleats. As today's Chargers continue to fight for the franchise's first NFL championship, their fans can't wait for lightning to strike again.

INDEX>